Contact Us:

✉ MyBibleWorkbooks@gmail.com

📷 Projectkingdomcome

f Projectkingdomcome

PROJECT KINGDOM COME
ISBN 978-1-961786-12-7

Get The Entire Workbook Series!

SCAN ME

THE BOOK OF
GENESIS
BIBLE-BASED WORKBOOK

...male and female He created them. Genesis 1:27

Take an adventure into the amazing Book of Genesis and test your knowledge as you go!

PROJECT KINGDOM COME

THE BOOKS OF
EXODUS & JOSHUA
BIBLE-BASED WORKBOOK

See, stand still! Joshua 10:12

Take an adventure into the amazing Books of Exodus and Joshua and test your knowledge as you go!

PROJECT KINGDOM COME

THE BOOKS OF
I & II SAMUEL
BIBLE-BASED WORKBOOK

And they anointed David king over the house of Judah. 2nd Samuel 2:4

Take an adventure into the amazing Books of 1st and 2nd Samuel and test your knowledge as you go!

PROJECT KINGDOM COME

THE BOOKS OF
I & II KINGS
BIBLE-BASED WORKBOOK

and he shall come and sit on my throne and reign be king. 1st Kings 1:35

Take an adventure into the amazing Books of 1st and 2nd Kings and test your knowledge as you go!

PROJECT KINGDOM COME

THE BOOKS OF
ESTHER & RUTH
BIBLE-BASED WORKBOOK

And she obtained grace and favor in his sight. Esther 2:17

Take an adventure into the amazing Books of Esther and Ruth and test your knowledge as you go!

PROJECT KINGDOM COME

THE BOOKS OF
DANIEL & JOB
BIBLE-BASED WORKBOOK

they brought Daniel and threw him into the lions' den. Daniel 6:16

Take an adventure into the amazing Books of Daniel and Job and test your knowledge as you go!

PROJECT KINGDOM COME

THE BOOK OF
MATTHEW
BIBLE-BASED WORKBOOK

Behold a virgin shall be with child. Matthew 1:23

Take an adventure into the amazing Book of Matthew and test your knowledge as you go!

PROJECT KINGDOM COME

THE BOOK OF
MARK
BIBLE-BASED WORKBOOK

Let us go into the next towns, that I may preach there also. Mark 1:38

Take an adventure into the amazing Book of Mark and test your knowledge as you go!

PROJECT KINGDOM COME

THE BOOK OF
LUKE
BIBLE-BASED WORKBOOK

...there they crucified Him. Luke 23:33

Take an adventure into the amazing Book of Luke and test your knowledge as you go!

PROJECT KINGDOM COME

THE BOOK OF
JOHN
BIBLE-BASED WORKBOOK

I am the resurrection and the life. John 11:25

Take an adventure into the amazing Book of John and test your knowledge as you go!

PROJECT KINGDOM COME

THE BOOK OF
ACTS
BIBLE-BASED WORKBOOK

In the name of Jesus Christ of Nazareth, rise up and walk. Acts 3:6

Take an adventure into the amazing Book of Acts and test your knowledge as you go!

PROJECT KINGDOM COME

THE BOOK OF
REVELATION
BIBLE-BASED WORKBOOK

Look, He is coming with the clouds, and every eye will see Him. Revelation 1:7

Take an adventure into the amazing Book of Revelation and test your knowledge as you go!

PROJECT KINGDOM COME

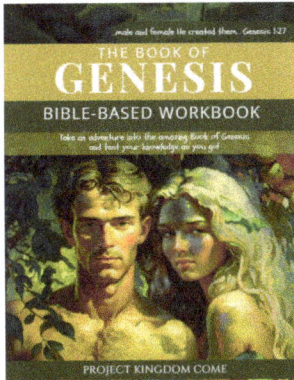

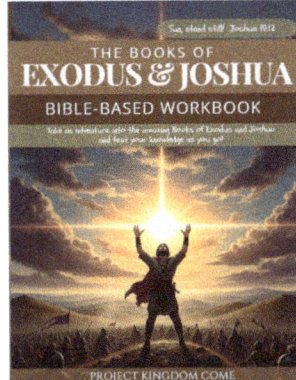

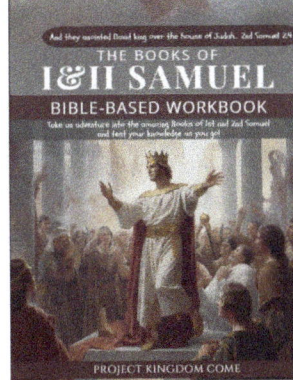

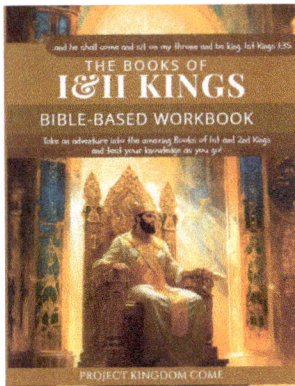

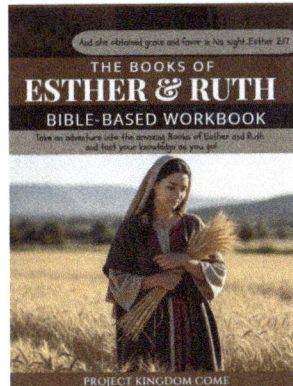

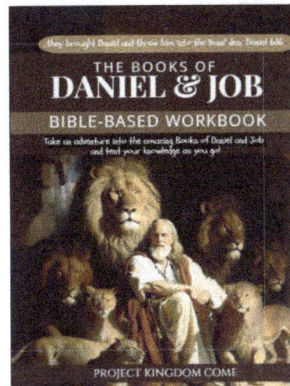

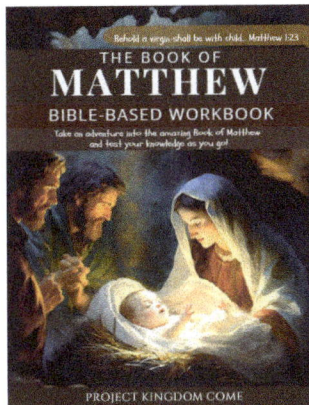

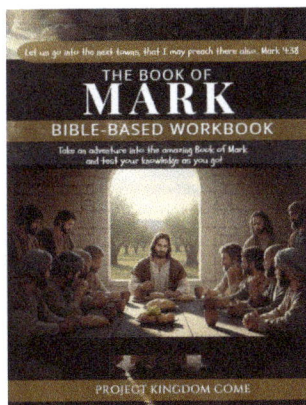

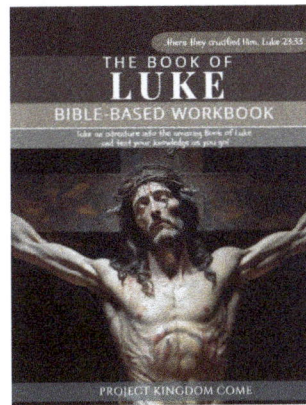

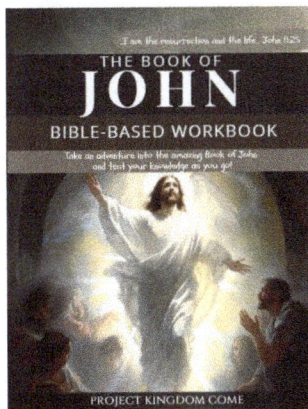

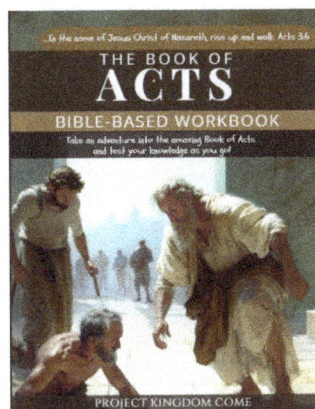

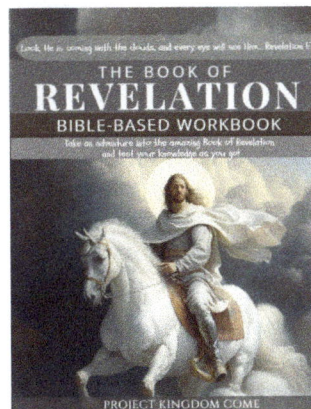

WWW.MYBIBLEWORKBOOKS.COM

PROJECT KINGDOM COME
Spread the Word

This workbook belongs to:

_____

_____

_____

Leave your mark!

HOW TO USE THIS WORKBOOK

This workbook is designed to help young people explore the treasures in God's Word while having fun, growing in faith, and learning how to search the Scriptures for life's answers.

Here is what you will find inside:

Multiple Choice Questions
Each question comes directly from Scripture and includes a reference verse to help with locating the answer in the Bible. If possible, use a physical Bible to search for the answers.

Weekly Segments
Questions are grouped in weekly categories that could also be completed in a shorter or longer time frame.

Weekly Memory Verses
At the start of every week is a Bible verse to memorize. Each day of that week will repeat that memory verse with a chance to test memorization at the end of the week.

Certificate of Completion
At the end of the workbook, please find a Certificate of Achievement, ready for the child's name and parent or teacher's signature. Celebrate the accomplishment of studying an entire book in the Bible!

Answer Key
The workbook contains an answer key to serve as a support tool for parents or teachers reviewing the responses.

Recommendation for Parents and/or Teachers: Review the responses with your child or student and discuss lessons learned or interesting insights, to improve the child's retention and enrichment in the knowledge of God's word.

You can do all things through Christ who gives you strength!
Philippians 4:13

SAMPLE QUESTION...
HOW TO USE THIS WORKBOOK

Reading the reference verse will always lead you to the correct answer!

In the beginning, God created: (Genesis 1:1)

A The Heavens and the Earth
B. Heaven and Earth
C. Heaven only
D. Earth only

The number that comes after the book is the 'Chapter'

This is the name of a book in the Bible

Joshua 1:8

The number after the chapter is the 'Verse'

NOW TEST YOURSELF! FIND JOSHUA CHAPTER 1 VERSE 8 IN YOUR BIBLE!

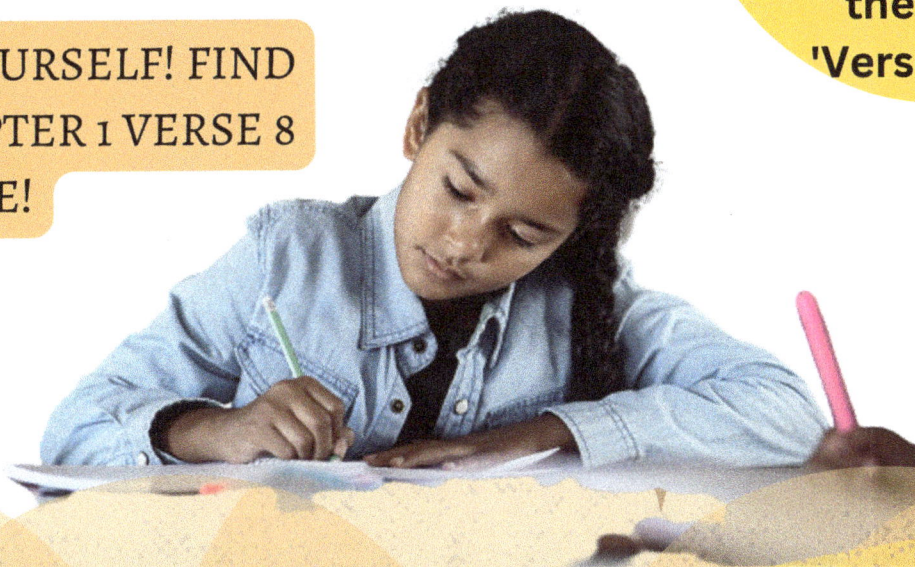

INTRODUCTION: THE BOOK OF GENESIS

The Book of Beginnings

Genesis is the first book of the Bible and the very beginning of God's incredible story of creation. The word Genesis means **"beginning"** — and that's exactly what this book is all about!

In Genesis, we learn how God created the heavens and the earth, made animals and oceans, people and planets — and said it was all **"very good."** But we also see how sin entered the world and how God began His plan to **deliver and bless His** people.

As you go through Genesis, you will meet some amazing people like **Adam and Eve, Noah, Abraham, Isaac, Jacob, and Joseph.** Some made mistakes, others showed great faith, but God never gave up on them, and He will not give up on you!

As you journey through Genesis, you will discover:

- **God is the Creator of everything**
- **God keeps His promises**
- **God can use anyone, even imperfect people**
- **God is writing a bigger story — and you're part of it!**

So grab your Bible and your pencil, and let's discover how it all began!

"In the beginning, God created the heavens and the earth." — Genesis 1:1

WEEK 1

> **1. What did God create on the first day?**
> **(Genesis 1:3-5)**
>
> A. The land and the sea
> B. Day and night
> C. The sun and the moon
> D. All living creatures

> **2. On what day did God create plants and trees?**
> **(Genesis 1: 11-13)**
>
> A. First Day
> B. Second Day
> C. Third Day
> D. Sixth Day

WEEK 1 MEMORY VERSE: GENESIS 1:1
In the beginning, God created the heavens and the earth.

WEEK 1

3. What great lights did God create on the fourth day? (Genesis 1:16-19)

A. The sun (greater light) and the moon (lesser light)
B. The day and the night
C. The moon and 12 stars
D. The sun alone

4. What did God say when He blessed the sea creatures and birds? (Genesis 1:21-22)

A. Fly high in the sky and make your nests in the trees
B. Be fruitful and increase in number
C. Do not worship any other god
D. Make the earth beautiful

WEEK 1 MEMORY VERSE: GENESIS 1:1

In the beginning, God created the heavens and the earth.

WEEK 1

5. **How did God create things for the first six days?**
(Genesis 1: 3,6,9,14,20,24)

A. By speaking them into existence
B. By dreaming about them
C. By using His angels to follow His commands
D. By making a wish on a shooting star

6. **Why was the creation of man more special than everything else? (Genesis 1:26-28)**

A. Man was created in God's image and likeness
B. Man was given authority to rule over all creation
C. Both A and B
D. None of the above

WEEK 1 MEMORY VERSE: GENESIS 1:1
In the beginning, God created the heavens and the earth.

WEEK 1

7. **Why did God bless the Seventh day and make it holy? (Genesis 2:2-3)**

A. Because He rested on the seventh day
B. Because He created man on the seventh day
C. Because it was the most beautiful day
D. Because it was the least stressful

8. **What did God use to make man? (Genesis 2:7)**

A. Clouds
B. Water
C. Feathers from birds
D. The dust of the ground

WEEK 1 MEMORY VERSE: GENESIS 1:1
In the beginning, God created the heavens and the earth.

WEEK 1

9. How did man become a living being? (Genesis 2:7)

A. God breathed into his nostrils
B. God sent the wind to blow on him
C. God told him to start breathing
D. He started breathing on his own

10. What is the name of the garden where God placed man? (Genesis 2:15)

A. Garden of Adam
B. Garden of Eve
C. Garden of Eden
D. Garden of Creation

WEEK 1 MEMORY VERSE: GENESIS 1:1
In the beginning, God created the heavens and the earth.

WEEK 1

11. **Which tree did God command man not to eat from? (Genesis 2:17)**

A. The Tree of Life and Victory
B. The Tree of the Knowledge of Good and Evil
C. The fig tree
D. The apple tree

12. **What did God say would happen if man ate from the forbidden tree? (Genesis 2:17)**

A. He would die
B. He would become wise
C. He would lose his wife
D. He would become like God

WEEK 1 MEMORY VERSE: GENESIS 1:1
In the beginning, God created the heavens and the earth.

13. What is the name of the first man God created? (Genesis 2:19-20)

A. Jesus
B. Moses
C. Abraham
D. Adam

14. Which part of man's body did God use to create the woman? (Genesis 2:21-22)

A. Hair
B. Nails
C. Rib
D. Blood

WEEK 1 MEMORY VERSE: GENESIS 1:1
In the beginning, God created the heavens and the earth.

KEEP GOING, YOU'RE DOING GREAT!

I am fearfully and wonderfully made by God
(Psalm 139:14)

Great job completing the week!

Did you memorize the daily verse?
Test yourself by writing it here...

_____

_____

_____

_____

_____

Use this space to draw a scene from the Bible or reflect on something you learned, felt, or like...

WEEK 2

15. Which animal tricked the woman into disobeying God? (Genesis 3:1-5)

A. Lion
B. Donkey
C. Serpent
D. Cow

16. Where was Adam when the woman was tempted? (Genesis 3:6)

A. He was sleeping
B. He had traveled
C. He was talking to God
D. He was with her

WEEK 2 MEMORY VERSE: GENESIS 2:18

And the Lord God said, "It is not good that man should be alone; I will make him a helper comparable to him."

WEEK 2

<<<<< >>>>>

"

17. How did the serpent deceive the woman? (Genesis 3:4)

A. He told her to leave her husband
B. He told her she would not die
C. He told her to cut down the tree
D. He told her Adam had lied

"

18. What punishment did the serpent receive for deceiving the woman? (Genesis 3:14-15)

A. He would crawl on his belly and eat dust
B. There would be enmity between him and the woman's offspring
C. He would ultimately be crushed by the woman's offspring
D. All the above

WEEK 2 MEMORY VERSE: GENESIS 2:18
And the Lord God said, "It is not good that man should be alone; I will make him a helper comparable to him."

WEEK 2

19. What punishment did the woman receive for her disobedience? (Genesis 3:16)

A. She would never be friends with God
B. She would have to crawl on her belly
C. She would have pain during childbirth
D. She was not punished, only Adam was

20. What punishment did the man receive for his disobedience? (Genesis 3:17-19)

A. The ground was cursed because of him
B. The ground would produce thorns for him
C. He would work hard and sweat for his food
D. All the above

WEEK 2 MEMORY VERSE: GENESIS 2:18
And the Lord God said, "It is not good that man should be alone; I will make him a helper comparable to him."

WEEK 2

21. What name did Adam give his wife?
(Genesis 3:20)

A. Sarah
B. Esther
C. Rebecca
D. Eve

22. Why was Cain unhappy with his brother Abel?
(Genesis 4: 4-5)

A. Because Abel was not helping him on the farm
B. Because God accepted Abel's offering and not Cain's
C. Because Cain wanted Abel to share his offering
D. Because Abel was a proud man

WEEK 2 MEMORY VERSE: GENESIS 2:18
And the Lord God said, "It is not good that man should be alone; I will make him a helper comparable to him."

WEEK 2

23. **What evil thing did Cain do to his brother?**
(Genesis 4:8)

A. He killed Abel's animals
B. He stole Abel's offering
C. He killed his brother Abel
D. He lied about Abel to God

24. **Which of the following is true about Enoch?**
(Genesis 5:24)

A. Enoch was one of Adam's sons
B. Enoch walked faithfully with God, and then he was no more because God took him away
C. Enoch did not die. God took him away
D. Both B and C

WEEK 2 MEMORY VERSE: GENESIS 2:18
And the Lord God said, "It is not good that man should be alone; I will make him a helper comparable to him."

WEEK 2

<<<<< >>>>>

"

25. What happened when the sons of God saw that the daughters of men were beautiful?
(Genesis 6:1-4)

A. They married any of the daughters they wanted
B. They had children with them called Nephilim
C. The Nephilim were on the earth in those days and afterward
D. All the above

"

26. Why did God instruct Noah to build an ark?
(Genesis 6:17)

A. Because God was about to destroy the earth with a flood
B. Because Noah was a carpenter
C. Because floods were common in that region
D. Because Noah's old ark needed repair

WEEK 2 MEMORY VERSE: GENESIS 2:18
And the Lord God said, "It is not good that man should be alone; I will make him a helper comparable to him."

WEEK 2

〈〈〈〈〈   〉〉〉〉〉

27. Why did God want to destroy the earth?
(Genesis 6:11-13)

A. To show His might
B. Because the earth was full of sin and violence
C. Because there was too much suffering
D. Because He wanted to create two earths

28. What instructions did God give Noah?
(Genesis 6: 18-21)

A. Bring two of every animal, male and female
B. Go into the ark with your wife, your sons, and their wives
C. Store food inside the ark
D. All the above

WEEK 2 MEMORY VERSE: GENESIS 2:18
And the Lord God said, "It is not good that man should be alone; I will make him a helper comparable to him."

"Like Noah, I have found grace in the sight of the Lord (Genesis 6:8)"

Great job completing the week!

Did you memorize the daily verse?
Test yourself by writing it here...

_____

_____

_____

_____

_____

Use this space to draw a scene from the Bible or reflect
on something you learned, felt or experienced...

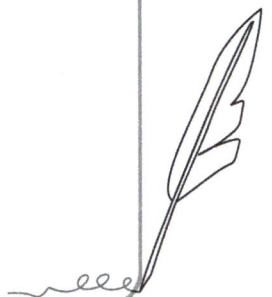

WEEK 3

<<<<< **WEEK 3** >>>>>

29. For how long did it rain in the days of Noah? (Genesis 7:4)

A. 7 days
B. 2 weeks
C. 30 days and nights
D. 40 days and 40 nights

30. What did God do after the flood? (Genesis 9:11-15)

A. God promised never to destroy all life with a flood again
B. God placed a rainbow in the sky as a covenant
C. Both A and B
D. None of the above

WEEK 3 MEMORY VERSE: GENESIS 15:6
And Abram believed the LORD, and the LORD counted him as righteous because of his faith.

31. Which of the following instructions did God give Abram? (Genesis 12:1)

A. Take his nephew Lot to a foreign land
B. Go from Canaan to Ur
C. Wait in Ur until the famine was over
D. Leave his country, people, and father's house and go to a new land

32. How old was Abram when he left his country? (Genesis 12:4)

A. 50 years old
B. 75 years old
C. 99 years old
D. 125 years old

WEEK 3 MEMORY VERSE: GENESIS 15:6
And Abram believed the LORD, and the LORD counted him as righteous because of his faith.

WEEK 3 «««« »»»»»

33. What is the name of the priest that blessed Abram? (Genesis 14:18-19)

A. Melchizedek, King of Salem
B. Elijah the Tishbite
C. Moses
D. Aaron

34. What did Abram give to God's priest? (Genesis 14:20)

A. A tenth of everything he had
B. Only what he was comfortable giving
C. Half of everything he had
D. Nothing

WEEK 3 MEMORY VERSE: GENESIS 15:6
And Abram believed the LORD, and the LORD counted him as righteous because of his faith.

35. What promise did God make to Abram?
(Genesis 15:5)

A. He would never die
B. He would be king of the Jews
C. He would have descendants as many as the stars
D. That he would inherit the land of Canaan

36. What did Sarai do when she realized she couldn't have children? (Genesis 16:1-4)

A. She gave Abram her Egyptian slave, Hagar, to bear children for her
B. She took one of Lot's children
C. She found a baby in a basket
D. She stole her neighbor's child

WEEK 3 MEMORY VERSE: GENESIS 15:6
And Abram believed the LORD, and the LORD counted him as righteous because of his faith.

37. Why did Hagar run away from Sarai? (Genesis 16:5-6)

A. She was tired of working
B. Sarai mistreated her
C. Sarai wanted to steal her child
D. She had stolen from Sarai

38. What is the name of Hagar and Abram's child? (Genesis 16:11)

A. Canaan
B. Isaac
C. Ishmael
D. Esau

WEEK 3 MEMORY VERSE: GENESIS 15:6
And Abram believed the LORD, and the LORD counted him as righteous because of his faith.

39. What name did God change Abram's name to?
(Genesis 17:5)

A. Canaan

B. Isaac

C. Abraham

D. Ishmael

40. What name did God change Sarai's name to?
(Genesis 17:15)

A. Rebecca

B. Hagar

C. Mary

D. Sarah

WEEK 3 MEMORY VERSE: GENESIS 15:6

And Abram believed the LORD, and the LORD counted him as righteous because of his faith.

"

41. How old were Abraham and Sarah when God promised to give them a son? (Genesis 17:17)

A. Abraham was 150 and Sarah was 100
B. Abraham was 75 and Sarah was 50
C. Abraham was 50 and Sarah was 25
D. Abraham was 100 and Sarah was 90

"

42. Why did God destroy the cities of Sodom and Gomorrah? (Genesis 18:20)

A. Because there was so much sin in Sodom & Gomorrah
B. Because the people rejected Abraham's message
C. Because nothing could survive in Sodom & Gomorrah
D. Because God wanted to give the land to Abraham

WEEK 3 MEMORY VERSE: GENESIS 15:6
And Abram believed the LORD, and the LORD counted him as righteous because of his faith.

Jehovah Jireh is my Provider. Just like Abraham, I trust that the Lord will provide for my every need

Genesis 22:14

Great job completing the week!

**Did you memorize the daily verse?
Test yourself by writing it here...**

_____

_____

_____

_____

_____

**Use this space to draw a scene from the Bible or reflect
on something you learned, felt or experienced...**

43. What is the lowest number of righteous people God agreed to spare the city for?
(Genesis 18:26-32)

A. 45

B. 20

C. 10

D. 3

44. Who did Lot try to save, but they thought he was joking? (Genesis 19:14)

A. His parents

B. His wife

C. His sons-in-law

D. His neighbors

WEEK 4 MEMORY VERSE: GENESIS 21:1
And the Lord visited Sarah as he had said, and the Lord did unto Sarah as he had spoken.

45. What happened to Lot's wife when she disobeyed the angel's instructions and looked back? (Genesis 19:26)

A. She got lost in the wilderness
B. She became blind from the fire
C. She froze in fear
D. She turned into a pillar of salt

46. What lie did Abraham tell about his wife, Sarah? (Genesis 20:2)

A. He said she was his sister
B. He said she was a queen
C. He said she had two sons
D. He said she was his mother

WEEK 4 MEMORY VERSE: GENESIS 21:1
And the Lord visited Sarah as he had said, and the Lord did unto Sarah as he had spoken.

47. Where did Hagar's son live, and what did he become when he grew up? (Genesis 21:20)

A. He lived in Abraham's house and became a farmer
B. He lived in the wilderness and became an archer
C. He lived in Pharaoh's house and became a priest
D. He lived in Canaan and became a shepherd

48. How did God test Abraham's faith? (Genesis 22:1-2)

A. He asked Abraham to give away all his wealth
B. He told Abraham to sacrifice his wife
C. He asked Abraham to leave Sarah
D. He asked Abraham to sacrifice his only son Isaac as a burnt offering

WEEK 4 MEMORY VERSE: GENESIS 21:1
And the Lord visited Sarah as he had said, and the Lord did unto Sarah as he had spoken.

49. What animal did God provide for Abraham to use as a burnt offering? (Genesis 22:9-13)

A. Cow

B. Ram

C. Dove

D. Bear

50. What promise did God make to Abraham for his willingness to sacrifice Isaac? (Genesis 22:15-18)

A. That his descendants would be as many as the stars and the sand

B. That he would become the strongest man in Canaan

C. That he would receive great riches

D. That he would be made king of Israel

WEEK 4 MEMORY VERSE: GENESIS 21:1
And the Lord visited Sarah as he had said, and the Lord did unto Sarah as he had spoken.

WEEK 4

51. **What is the name of Isaac's wife?**
(Genesis 24:66-67)

A. Leah

B. Rachel

C. Rebekah

D. Esther

52. **What are the names of Isaac's twins?**
(Genesis 25:24-26)

A. Cain and Abel

B. Esau and Jacob

C. Abraham and Moses

D. David and Jonathan

WEEK 4 MEMORY VERSE: GENESIS 21:1
And the Lord visited Sarah as he had said, and the Lord did unto Sarah as he had spoken.

53. What did Esau receive in exchange for his birthright? (Genesis 25:29-34)

A. A bowl of soup/stew
B. Thousands of cows and goats
C. A blessing from Isaac
D. A large piece of land

54 . What is the name of the third well Isaac dug, and what is the meaning of the name? (Genesis 26:22)

A. Rehema, which means "mercy"
B. Gerar, which means "a place to rest"
C. Beersheba, which means "oath"
D. Rehoboth, which means "the Lord has given us room"

WEEK 4 MEMORY VERSE: GENESIS 21:1
And the Lord visited Sarah as he had said, and the Lord did unto Sarah as he had spoken.

55. How did Jacob steal Esau's blessing?
(Genesis 27:1-35)

A. He wore goatskins to appear hairy

B. His mother Rebekah helped him deceive Isaac

C. He pretended to be Esau and tricked his father

D. All the above

56. How did Jacob encounter God in a dream?
(Genesis 28:10-16)

A. He saw a stairway from earth to heaven

B. He saw angels ascending and descending

C. He saw the Lord standing above the ladder

D. All the above

WEEK 4 MEMORY VERSE: GENESIS 21:1
And the Lord visited Sarah as he had said, and the Lord did unto
Sarah as he had spoken.

I believe and therefore all things are possible for me
(Mark 9:23)

Great job completing the week!

Did you memorize the daily verse?
Test yourself by writing it here...

_____

_____

_____

_____

_____

Use this space to draw a scene from the Bible or reflect
on something you learned, felt or experienced...

57. What did God say to Jacob in the dream? (Genesis 28:13)

A. "Why did you lie to Esau?"
B. "Go back to your father's house."
C. "I am the Lord, the God of Abraham and Isaac. I will give this land to you and your descendants."
D. "I am the Lord and I'm not pleased with your lies."

58. How did Jacob mark the place where he encountered God? (Genesis 28: 18-19)

A. He cut trees to build an altar
B. He built a house and called it Canaan
C. He made an altar with the stone he slept on and named the place Bethel
D. He buried treasure there

WEEK 5 MEMORY VERSE: GENESIS 35:3

Then let us arise and go up to Bethel; and I will make an altar there to God, who answered me in the day of my distress and has been with me in the way which I have gone.

59. What vow did Jacob make to God?
(Genesis 28:20-22)

A. That the Lord would be his God

B. That he would set up a memorial stone

C. That he would give God a tenth of all he received

D. All the above

60. How many years did Jacob work for Laban in total? (Genesis 29:16-30 and Genesis 31:41)

A. 20 years

B. 17 years

C. 6 years

D. 1 month

WEEK 5 MEMORY VERSE: GENESIS 35:3

Then let us arise and go up to Bethel; and I will make an altar there to God, who answered me in the day of my distress and has been with me in the way which I have gone.

61. How did Laban deceive Jacob?
(Genesis 29:25-26)

A. He refused to give him a wife
B. He hid Jacob's gold and silver
C. He gave him Leah instead of Rachel
D. He made Jacob marry someone from a different country

62. Which of the following is NOT one of Leah's sons? (Genesis 29:31-35)

A. Joseph
B. Simeon
C. Levi
D. Judah

WEEK 5 MEMORY VERSE: GENESIS 35:3
Then let us arise and go up to Bethel; and I will make an altar there to God, who answered me in the day of my distress and has been with me in the way which I have gone.

63. What happened when Jacob wrestled with an angel of God? (Genesis 32:24-32)

A. God changed his name to Israel

B. His hip was dislocated

C. Both A and B

D. He was struck by lightning

64. Where did God instruct Jacob to live and build an altar? (Genesis 35:1)

A. Canaan

B. Egypt

C. Goshen

D. Bethel

WEEK 5 MEMORY VERSE: GENESIS 35:3

Then let us arise and go up to Bethel; and I will make an altar there to God, who answered me in the day of my distress and has been with me in the way which I have gone.

65. **What instructions did Jacob give to his household before building an altar to the Lord? (Genesis 35:2)**

A. Get rid of all foreign gods

B. Purify themselves

C. Change their clothes

D. All the above

66. **How many sons did Jacob have? (Genesis 35:22)**

A. 6

B. 12

C. 11

D. 13

WEEK 5 MEMORY VERSE: GENESIS 35:3
Then let us arise and go up to Bethel; and I will make an altar there to God, who answered me in the day of my distress and has been with me in the way which I have gone.

67. What are the names of Rachel's sons?
(Genesis 35:24)

A. Joseph and Judah
B. Dan and Naphtali
C. Joseph and Benjamin
D. Gad and Asher

68. What is Esau's other name?
(Genesis 36:1)

A. Edom
B. Amalek
C. Jacob
D. Israel

WEEK 5 MEMORY VERSE: GENESIS 35:3
Then let us arise and go up to Bethel; and I will make an altar there to God, who answered me in the day of my distress and has been with me in the way which I have gone.

69. How old was Joseph when his brothers sold him? (Genesis 37:2)

A. 17 years old

B. 25 years old

C. 30 years old

D. 40 years old

70. Which son did Jacob (Israel) love the most? (Genesis 37:3)

A. Reuben

B. Benjamin

C. Joseph

D. He favored all the firstborn equally

WEEK 5 MEMORY VERSE: GENESIS 35:3

Then let us arise and go up to Bethel; and I will make an altar there to God, who answered me in the day of my distress and has been with me in the way which I have gone.

The Lord is my shepherd, I shall not want. He makes me lie down in green pastures and leads me beside the still waters (Psalms 23:1-2)

Great job completing the week!

Did you memorize the daily verse?
Test yourself by writing it here...

_____

_____

_____

_____

_____

_____

Use this space to draw a scene from the Bible or reflect
on something you learned, felt or experienced...

WEEK 6

71. Why did Joseph's brothers hate him? (Genesis 37:3-5)

A. He was young and annoying
B. He was their father's favorite
C. They didn't like his dreams
D. Both B and C

72. Which of the following is true about Joseph's dreams? (Genesis 37:5-10)

A. His brothers' bundles of grain bowed to his
B. The sun, moon, and eleven stars bowed to him
C. He dreamed he was famous
D. Both A and B

WEEK 6 MEMORY VERSE: GENESIS 50:20
You intended to harm me, but God intended it for good to accomplish what is now being done, the saving of many lives.

WEEK 6

73. What did Joseph's brothers do to him before selling him? (Genesis 37:23-28)

A. They removed his robe and threw him in a pit
B. They bound his hands and feet
C. They left him in the desert to die
D. Both B and C

74. What lie did Joseph's brothers tell their father? (Genesis 37:31-33)

A. They said Joseph ran away from home
B. They dipped his robe in blood and told their father a wild animal had killed him
C. They told their father Joseph had fallen off a cliff
D. They said Joseph had gotten lost while looking for his brothers

WEEK 6 MEMORY VERSE: GENESIS 50:20
You intended to harm me, but God intended it for good to accomplish what is now being done, the saving of many lives.

WEEK 6

75. Where was Joseph sold by the Midianites?
(Genesis 37:36)

A. To Pharaoh in Bethlehem

B. To Potiphar in Egypt

C. To Esau in Shechem

D. He was not sold

76. What is the name of Tamar's twin son who had a scarlet thread tied around his hand?
(Genesis 38:27-30)

A. Jacob

B. Esau

C. Perez

D. Zerah

WEEK 6 MEMORY VERSE: GENESIS 50:20
You intended to harm me, but God intended it for good to accomplish what is now being done, the saving of many lives.

WEEK 6

> **77. In what ways did God bless Joseph while he was in Potiphar's house?**
> **(Genesis 39:1-6)**
>
> A. Potiphar's entire household was blessed because of Joseph
> B. Joseph succeeded in everything he did
> C. Potiphar put Joseph in charge of all he owned
> D. All of the above

> **78. While in jail, Joseph interpreted dreams for which two people? (Genesis 40:1-23)**
>
> A. The king's messenger and chef
> B. The chief cupbearer and the chief baker
> C. The chief dancer and Potiphar
> D. Two prison guards

WEEK 6 MEMORY VERSE: GENESIS 50:20
You intended to harm me, but God intended it for good to accomplish what is now being done, the saving of many lives.

WEEK 6

> ## 79. Which of the following were Pharaoh's dreams? (Genesis 41:1-7)
>
> A. Seven thin cows ate seven fat cows
> B. Seven thin heads of grain swallowed seven healthy ones
> C. Birds were eating bread out of three baskets
> D. Both A and B

> ## 80. What was Joseph's interpretation of Pharaoh's dreams? (Genesis 41:28-30)
>
> A. Animals would eat each other for 7 years
> B. Plants would consume each other for 7 years
> C. There would be 7 years of abundance followed by 7 years of famine
> D. There would be 7 years of peace followed by 7 years of war

WEEK 6 MEMORY VERSE: GENESIS 50:20
You intended to harm me, but God intended it for good to accomplish what is now being done, the saving of many lives.

WEEK 6

81. What advice did Joseph give Pharaoh after interpreting his dreams? (Genesis 41:33-36)

A. Find a wise man to oversee Egypt
B. Collect food during the 7 years of plenty
C. Store and guard the food for the famine
D. All the above

82. Who did Pharaoh appoint to oversee Egypt? (Genesis 41:41-43)

A. Potiphar
B. Pharaoh's son
C. Joseph
D. Judah

WEEK 6 MEMORY VERSE: GENESIS 50:20
You intended to harm me, but God intended it for good to accomplish what is now being done, the saving of many lives.

WEEK 6

83. Why did Joseph's brothers come to Egypt? (Genesis 42:1-3)

A. There was a severe famine in Canaan
B. They were looking for Joseph
C. Food in Egypt was cheaper
D. They needed medicine for Jacob

84. What happened when Joseph's brothers arrived in Egypt? (Genesis 42:6-8)

A. They couldn't speak Egyptian
B. Joseph sent them away in anger
C. Joseph recognized them, but they didn't recognize him
D. They never arrived

WEEK 6 MEMORY VERSE: GENESIS 50:20
You intended to harm me, but God intended it for good to accomplish what is now being done, the saving of many lives.

God is working all things together for my good, because I love Him and I am called according to His purpose
(Romans 8:28)

Great job completing the week!

Did you memorize the daily verse?
Test yourself by writing it here...

_____

_____

_____

_____

_____

_____

Use this space to draw a scene from the Bible or reflect
on something you learned, felt or experienced...

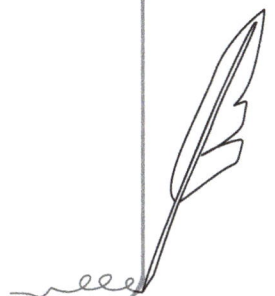

WEEK 7

85. Which one of Joseph's brothers was put in jail? (Genesis 42:22-24)

A. Rueben

B. Benjamin

C. Levi

D. Simeon

86. How did Joseph reveal himself to his brothers? (Genesis 45:1-5)

A. Pharaoh made the announcement to his brothers

B. Joseph sent a letter through a servant

C. Joseph asked everyone else to leave the room and told them himself

D. One of the Egyptian guards revealed it

WEEK 7 MEMORY VERSE: JOHN 1:12

But as many as received Him, to them He gave the right to become children of God, to those who believe in His name:

WEEK 7

87. What is the name of Joseph's wife? (Genesis 46:20)

A. Asenath, daughter of Potiphera
B. Bilhah, daughter of Esau
C. Ruth, daughter of Hiram
D. Zilpah, daughter of Levi

88. How many members of Jacob's family went with him to Egypt? (Genesis 46:27)

A. 40
B. 100
C. 12
D. 70

WEEK 7 MEMORY VERSE: JOHN 1:12
But as many as received Him, to them He gave the right to become children of God, to those who believe in His name:

WEEK 7

89. What is the name of the land in Egypt where Jacob's family settled? (Genesis 47:1-6)

A. Goshen
B. Canaan
C. Israel
D. Bethel

90. Which law did Joseph establish in Egypt? (Genesis 47:26)

A. Egyptians must bow to Pharaoh's image
B. A fifth of the harvest belonged to Pharaoh, except the land of the priests
C. Israelites must work for Egyptians
D. Pharaoh must free all slaves

WEEK 7 MEMORY VERSE: JOHN 1:12
But as many as received Him, to them He gave the right to become children of God, to those who believe in His name:

WEEK 7

91. How many years did Jacob live in Egypt? (Genesis 47:28)

A. 10
B. 15
C. 17
D. 21

92. What are the names of Joseph's sons? (Genesis 48:5)

A. Esau and Jacob
B. Benjamin and Manasseh
C. Manasseh and Ephraim
D. Ephraim and Canaan

WEEK 7 MEMORY VERSE: JOHN 1:12

But as many as received Him, to them He gave the right to become children of God, to those who believe in His name:

WEEK 7

93. What happened when Jacob crossed his hands while blessing Joseph's sons? (Genesis 48:17-19)

A. The younger son was blessed above the older

B. It was a mistake

C. He crossed them for comfort

D. Joseph was happy that Jacob had crossed his hands

94. Which of the following was NOT part of Jacob's blessing to Judah? (Genesis 49:8)

A. You will shine like the morning sun

B. Your brothers will praise you

C. Your hand will be on the neck of your enemies

D. Your father's sons will bow down to you

WEEK 7 MEMORY VERSE: JOHN 1:12

But as many as received Him, to them He gave the right to become children of God, to those who believe in His name:

WEEK 7

95. Where was Jacob buried?
(Genesis 49:29-30)

A. In Goshen
B. In Egypt
C. In Bethlehem
D. In a cave in the field of Ephron

96. How long did the Egyptians mourn the death of Jacob? (Genesis 50:1-3)

A. 70 days
B. 35 days
C. 40 days
D. 50 days

WEEK 7 MEMORY VERSE: JOHN 1:12
But as many as received Him, to them He gave the right to become children of God, to those who believe in His name:

WEEK 7

97. What did Joseph say to his brothers when they feared revenge? (Genesis 50:20)

A. May the Lord bless you
B. What goes around comes around
C. You intended to harm me, but God used it for good
D. To God be the glory for saving me

98. How old was Joseph when he died? (Genesis 50:26)

A. 130 years
B. 110 years old
C. 25 years old
D. 75 years old

WEEK 7 MEMORY VERSE: JOHN 1:12

But as many as received Him, to them He gave the right to become children of God, to those who believe in His name:

I am led by the Spirit of God, so I know without a doubt that I am a child of God!
(Romans 8:14)

Great job completing the week!

**Did you memorize the daily verse?
Test yourself by writing it here...**

_____

_____

_____

_____

_____

_____

**Use this space to draw a scene from the Bible or reflect
on something you learned, felt or experienced...**

Certificate of Completion

This Certificate Certifies That:

_____

Has Successfully Completed The Genesis Workbook!

Flo & Grace

_____

PARENT/TEACHER SIGNATURE

PROJECT KINGDOM COME

WOULD YOU LIKE TO ACCEPT JESUS INTO YOUR HEART?

THE BIBLE SAYS:

If you confess with your mouth that Jesus is Lord and believe in your heart that God has raised Him from the dead, you will be saved
(Romans 10:9)

SAY THE PRAYER BELOW OUT LOUD AND BELIEVE IT IN YOUR HEART!

Dear Lord Jesus,
I know that I am a sinner, and I ask for Your forgiveness.
I believe You died for my sins and rose from the dead.
I repent of my sins and invite You to come into my heart and life.
I want to trust and follow You as my Lord and Savior. Help me to live
for you for the rest of my life.
I am now a child of God, and I ask You to fill me with Your Holy Spirit.

In Jesus' Name I pray, Amen.

Congratulations!
If you have prayed this prayer, please let an adult know or
send an email to mybibleworkbooks@gmail.com

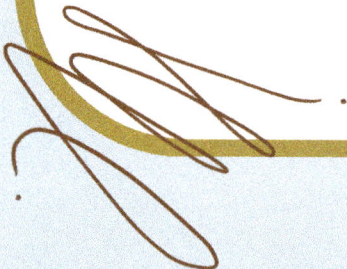

<u>ANSWER KEY:</u>

<<<<<   >>>>>

1.B	13.D	25.D
2.C	14.C	26.A
3.A	15.C	27.B
4.B	16.D	28.D
5.A	17.B	29.D
6.C	18.D	30.C
7.A	19.C	31.D
8.D	20.D	32.B
9.A	21.D	33.A
10. C	22.B	34. A
11. B	23.C	35. C
12. A	24.D	36. A

ANSWER KEY:

37.B	49.B	61.C
38.C	50.A	62.A
39.C	51.C	63.C
40.D	52.B	64.D
41.D	53.A	65.D
42.A	54.D	66.B
43.C	55.D	67.C
44.C	56.D	68.A
45.D	57.C	69.A
46.A	58.C	70.C
47.B	59.D	71.D
48.D	60.A	72.D

73.A

74.B

75.B

76.D

77.D

78.B

79.D

80.C

81.D

82.C

83.A

84.C

85.D

86.C

87.A

88.D

89.A

90.B

91.C

92.C

93.A

94.A

95.D

96.A

97.C

98.B

PLEASE GIVE US YOUR FEEDBACK!

Please send us your feedback on this workbook. We would love to hear what you enjoyed most, and ways you think it could be improved!

Please Send an email to: MyBibleWorkbooks@gmail.com, or leave us a comment on one of our social media pages.

✉ MyBibleWorkbooks@gmail.com

📷 Projectkingdomcome

f Projectkingdomcome

SCAN ME

"

And I am certain that God, who began the good work within you, will continue His work until it is finally finished on the day when Christ Jesus returns.

Philippians 1:6

"

DRAW HERE

DRAW HERE

DRAW HERE

DRAW HERE

DRAW HERE

www.ingramcontent.com/pod-product-compliance
Lightning Source LLC
Chambersburg PA
CBHW061410090426
42740CB00026B/3494